UNDAUNTED

UNDAUNTED

The Wild Life of Biruté Mary Galdikas and Her Fearless Quest to Save Orangutans

ANITA SILVEY

Foreword by Biruté Mary Galdikas

NATIONAL GEOGRAPHIC

WASHINGTON, D.C.

Since 1888, the National Geographic Society has funded more than 12,000 research, exploration, and preservation projects around the world. The Society receives funds from National Geographic Partners, LLC, funded in part by your purchase. A portion of the proceeds from this book supports this vital work. To learn more, visit natgeo.com/info.

NATIONAL GEOGRAPHIC and Yellow Border Design are trademarks of the National Geographic Society, used under license.

For more information, visit nationalgeographic.com, call 1-800-647-5463, or write to the following address:

National Geographic Partners
1145 17th Street N.W.
Washington, D.C. 20036-4688 U.S.A.

Visit us online at nationalgeographic.com/books

For librarians and teachers: ngchildrensbooks.org

More for kids from National Geographic: natgeokids.com

National Geographic Kids magazine inspires children to explore their world with fun yet educational articles on animals, science, nature, and more. Using fresh storytelling and amazing photography, *Nat Geo Kids* shows kids ages 6 to 14 the fascinating truth about the world—and why they should care.
kids.nationalgeographic.com/subscribe

For information about special discounts for bulk purchases, please contact National Geographic Books Special Sales: specialsales@natgeo.com

For rights or permissions inquiries, please contact National Geographic Books Subsidiary Rights: bookrights@natgeo.com

Library of Congress Cataloging-in-Publication Data

Names: Silvey, Anita, author. I National Geographic Kids (Firm), publisher. I National Geographic Society (U.S.)
Title: Undaunted / by Anita Silvey.
Description: Washington, DC : National Geographic Kids, [2019] I Audience: Age 8-12. I Audience: Grade 4 to 6.
Identifiers: LCCN 2018036051I ISBN 9781426333569 (hardcover) I ISBN 9781426333576 (hardcover)
Subjects: LCSH: Galdikas, Biruté Marija Filomena. I Women primatologists--Biography --Juvenile literature. I Orangutans--Behavior--Research--Borneo--Juvenile literature. I Orangutans--Behavior--Research--Indonesia--Sumatra--Juvenile literature
Classification: LCC QL31.G34 S55 2019 I DDC 599.88/3092 [B] --dc23
LC record available at https://lccn.loc.gov/2018036051

Designed by Marty Ittner

The publisher would like to thank everyone who made this book possible: Kate Hale, executive editor; Julide Dengel, art director; Sarah J. Mock, senior photo editor; Joan Gossett, production editorial manager; Paige Towler, associate editor; Kathryn Williams, associate editor; Avery Naughton, editorial assistant; Mike McNey, cartographer; and Anne LeongSon and Gus Tello, production designers. Special thanks also to the dedicated staff at Orangutan Foundation International for contributing their time and effort to this project.

PREVIOUS PAGES: Biruté Mary Galdikas explores the Bornean rain forest with an orphaned orangutan. When she started her research, she hand-raised orangutans at her camp, living alongside them and becoming a surrogate mother.

RIGHT: A young orangutan climbs a tree at Camp Leakey in Tanjung Puting National Park.

The paper used for this book is harvested sustainably and does not negatively impact orangutan habitats.

Printed in China
18/RRDS/1

Contents

Foreword

Biruté Mary Galdikas

While at a feeding station, Biruté is surrounded by several orangutans rescued from captivity. Since she arrived in Borneo nearly 50 years ago, Biruté and her staff have rehabilitated and released hundreds of former captive and orphaned orangutans back into the rain forest.

Ever since I was a small child, I was curious. I wanted to discover new paths through my favorite park and learn about nearly everything at school. But most often, I wondered about the very existence of human beings. Where did we come from? Who were our ancestors?

Some say that scientists are people who never lose their curiosity. When I began to study a certain species of the mysterious great ape, I started asking even *more* questions—and my life completely changed. Now, nearly 50 years later, I've dedicated most of my life to the rain forests of Indonesian Borneo and to its orangutans, showing the world what these animals are like and how, in some ways, they are not so different from us at all.

People are often curious about what my life is like. Some think my work is "glamorous." They see glossy photos of me walking in the lush green jungles of Borneo, following orangutans swinging through the trees. But these images don't show the sweat pouring down, the exhaustion, the illness, the hunger, and the thirst. While there is beauty in the rain forest, there are also endless rainstorms, stifling heat, hungry crocodiles, leeches, insects, and venomous creatures. Even so, wading up to my armpits from dawn to dusk in the black, acidic waters of these swamp forests while observing orangutans in the trees up above is the easy part.

The hard part is conservation. Orangutans are the most endangered great apes on Earth, and they are under threat from all sides—including destruction of their forests, climate change, and poachers. These animals and the places they call home need saving.

This is why I established Orangutan Foundation International, a nonprofit dedicated to preserving orangutans and their fragile ecosystems. My team and I do everything we can. Sometimes this means helping orangutans directly, such as rescuing individuals kept illegally as pets. Persuading angry owners to relinquish orangutan babies was—and still is—hard, but every orangutan life matters in the fight to save this species.

We also fight for conservation on a broader scale: saving and protecting the tropical rain forests—the orangutans' only home. We've fought raging wildfires and driven out illegal loggers, poachers, and miners who invaded our study area and Tanjung Puting, a national park we encouraged the government to establish. These threats are directed not only at animals and their habitats, but also at us. We have been physically assaulted. We have been taunted. We have had to be relentless. I've led police patrols to catch groups of illegal loggers and poachers. I have haunted government offices and politely confronted politicians and officials. I've written letters and proposals to cabinet ministers. I've endured endless meetings. If following wild orangutans in the swamps has not taught me patience, sitting in officials' waiting rooms certainly has. Eventually, most of the illegal logging and strip mining activities inside the park came to an end, but the threats outside the park have only escalated as development continues to extend deep into the rain forest.

While the future of these incredible great apes remains bleak, there is some hope. The population I study, now arguably the largest wild orangutan population in the world, is still here. And I hope that my story will inspire you, and others like you around the globe, so we can make sure these amazing animals continue to have a home for years to come.

Although my work has been filled with challenges—and I expect more will come—I am still here, undaunted. And I know that there are many other people who—just like me—are curious and asking questions. You too may want to take on challenges to save vital species like orangutans. Know that your road won't be easy and the fight will be hard, but the reward—helping save animals, habitats, and the Earth itself—will always be worth the battle.

First Contact

A large male orangutan, weighing at least 250 pounds (113 kg), ambled along the path, head down, unaware of everything around him. Then he stopped dead in his tracks. He stared and stared at the strange being less than 12 feet (4 m) ahead—a pale-faced creature with large hazel eyes. The narrow path, fenced in by tall ferns, did not leave room for both of them. Suddenly, with his coat blazing bright orange in the sunlight, the animal whirled around and vanished.

Standing silent, still, and expressionless, Biruté Mary Galdikas marveled at her first encounter, face-to-face, with a wild adult male orangutan.

"As far back as I can remember, I have been fascinated with human origins. I continually asked: How do humans fit into the universe? Who were our ancestors? ... Why do humans exist in the first place?"

CHAPTER 1

EXPLORER IN TRAINING

A Young Girl With a Passion for Nature

Long before Biruté Mary Galdikas first met the wild orangutans of Borneo, she always believed she'd been destined to be with them. Many seemingly unrelated incidents in her life led her to the remote rain forests and its inhabitants. "I was born to study orangutans," she wrote.

Biruté's journey began in Europe. Generations of her ancestors came from Lithuania, a small country on the Baltic Sea. With its picturesque landscape of peat bogs, gentle hills, and looming dark and dense forests, the country had been a peaceful place to live.

Biruté loved animals and exploration ever since she was a little girl. Here, she tracks orangutans by boat, with the help of locals and some orange-haired friends, within her 14-square-mile (36-sq-km) study area of Tanjung Puting in Indonesian Borneo.

Lithuania

Located on the shore of the Baltic Sea, today Lithuania is home to about three million people. The modern country came into being on February 16, 1918, near the end of the First World War. During World War II, Lithuania was occupied first by the Soviet Union and then by Nazi Germany. When the Soviet army first entered Lithuania, Biruté's family fled to Berlin, Germany, for safe harbor. By doing so, they escaped becoming one of the 780,000 Lithuanians who were arrested, deported to labor camps in Siberia, or lost their lives at the hands of the Soviets.

Lithuanians have always emphasized education. In the country today, 99.8 percent are literate by age 15; around 93 percent finish a college education, the highest education rate in the European Union. Choral singing, folklore, and dance are all valued in this culture. As Biruté said about her childhood, "Every week we went to church, a piano recital, a concert or an opera that was Lithuanian. The Lithuanian cultural events were nonstop."

FLEEING FROM WAR

The Soviet occupation of Lithuania during World War II wasn't actually the first time that Biruté's family had to leave their home. While Biruté's grandmother was Lithuanian, Biruté's grandfather was a Lithuanian American. During World War I, her grandparents were able to enter the United States for safe haven. It was there that they gave birth to Biruté's aunt Eugenie. After the war was over, the family moved back to Lithuania, which had just declared independence. They lived there peacefully for two decades before World War II began.

Refugees in a line stretching as far as the eye can see pull carts filled with their belongings in Berlin, Germany, during the summer of 1945.

But when Lithuania was occupied by the Soviet army in June 1940, the political situation changed dramatically. A successful farmer, Biruté's grandmother discovered that her name appeared on a list of those who would have their property seized and then be deported to a labor camp. Moving quickly, the entire family fled their country and joined Biruté's aunt Eugenie in Berlin, Germany. They each fit everything they could into one suitcase and left the country they loved.

Five years later, World War II ended, on May 8, 1945. The city of Berlin was split into different occupation zones: American, French, British, and Soviet. All foreigners who took refuge in Germany during the war now had to report to refugee camps. During her first month in the camp, Biruté's mother, Filomena, and father, Antanas, also Lithuanian, met at a dance. They fell in love and married. But the couple and their families didn't celebrate for long. While living in a camp controlled by the Soviet military, Filomena and Antanas worried that they might still be sent to a labor camp—the very thing that had made them flee Lithuania. So the day after the wedding, the new

Filomena and Antanas Galdikas pose for a photo with three-year-old Biruté on a family visit to High Park in Toronto, Canada.

couple, Biruté's mother's family, and 20 other wedding guests headed toward the area of Germany protected by the American army. They traveled on foot, dragging carts loaded with all their belongings.

In May 1946, Biruté was born in West Germany—a baby with no permanent home. Antanas and Filomena wanted to immigrate to America, as did many others, but the United States could only take in a certain number of refugees. So Biruté's parents instead chose Canada as a destination.

Antanas Galdikas found employment in Canada in the gold and copper mines. Soon, the rest of the family joined him and they moved to the city of Toronto. Filomena worked as a nurse, and it was there that Biruté's brother Vytas Anthony; sister, Aldona; and brother Al were born.

As a small child, Biruté adapted quickly to her new country while still honoring her family's heritage. The family worshipped in a Catholic Lithuanian church and joined Canadian Lithuanian organizations. On Saturdays, Biruté attended a special Lithuanian language school for many years. When she entered kindergarten, she did not speak English. On her first day, she could understand nothing the teacher or the other children said. Smart and determined, Biruté mastered English at age five, becoming bilingual. Not only did she know two languages, but she was also now immersed in two different cultures. She had already learned that "there is more than one way of looking at the world." That understanding served her well when she later went to live in Indonesia.

The family spent weekends enjoying picnics in the extensive Toronto parks or camping in the forests of Ontario. Biruté's mother constantly encouraged discussion about the

Curious George

On a field trip in first grade, Biruté discovered the Toronto Public Library and checked out her first book, *Curious George*.

Created by H. A. Rey, a World War II refugee named Hans originally from Germany, *Curious George* tells the story of a mischievous monkey and the man in the yellow hat who always saves him. With help from his wife, Margret, Hans drafted the first version of the book while on a long honeymoon in France. Originally the protagonist was named Fifi, a female character based on Margret Rey, and the pictures depicted Paris street scenes.

Barely escaping the Nazis when they entered France, the Reys rode bicycles out of Paris and eventually managed to get themselves and their manuscripts to New York. Grace Hogarth at Houghton Mifflin gave Hans a four-book contract to help support the Reys as wartime refugees. By the time Biruté discovered the *Curious George* books in the 1950s, the saga of the mischievous monkey had become a staple in public library collections. As well as sparking Biruté's interest in monkeys and apes, the book inspired her to became a voracious reader.

Toronto in the 1950s

The Canada of Biruté's childhood was a far cry from the war-torn Europe her family had fled. The 1950s found Canada booming as the country's economy grew and its population swelled. In Toronto, this led to the city expanding its suburbs, improving infrastructure, and building the Toronto subway—the first in Canada.

During this time period, cars became more affordable, more reliable, and more popular than ever before. Canadians began living farther from cities, and the suburbs of Toronto began to grow. These homes had more space and larger residences to fill with appliances and gadgets—including TVs. In the early 1950s, Toronto also got its first Canadian television station. Back then, TV was relatively new and expensive, but that didn't stop Canadians from tuning in. They watched Canadian originals, such as *Hockey Night* and the comedic duo Wayne and Shuster, as well as iconic American shows, including *Leave It to Beaver* and *I Love Lucy*.

After the war, immigrant communities like the one Biruté grew up in experienced this growth while keeping their own traditions alive, some of which could no longer be practiced freely in their home countries. The Lithuanian community in Canada tripled from 1941 to 1951. These newcomers came together to support one another, celebrate their culture, and host uniquely Lithuanian events, such as the Lithuanian Song Festival, which thrived in postwar Canada.

natural world. "We'd be walking somewhere and my mother would pick up a leaf that had fallen from a tree and then talk about it." But Biruté's own nature excursions when she was nine years old changed the course of her life. Two blocks away from her home, one of Canada's premier parks, High Park, stretched for 400 acres (162 ha). A third of the park remained in its natural state, with lush vegetation and virgin forests. Marked by deep ravines, small creeks, and ponds, the park not only provided Biruté with an opportunity to study the native plants and animals of the area, but it also sparked her imagination and curiosity.

Above: The postwar era—the time when Biruté was growing up—was a period of development for Toronto, Canada. By 1951, the city's population surged to more than a million people.

The Galdikas family sits for a photograph. Clockwise from top: Biruté's father, Antanas; brother (the older of two), Vytas; sister, Aldona; mother, Filomena; Biruté; and her second brother, Al.

In Grenadier Pond, she searched for tadpoles and turned over the rocks to locate blunt-snouted salamanders.

In streams gently flowing under willow trees, she spotted enormous land turtles and nesting mallard ducks.

At times in this vast and wild landscape, she imagined that she herself was an indigenous person on her way to a French trading fort. She was fascinated by the prehistory of the park—even back to the origins of humans there.

During these excursions, Biruté decided she wanted to be an explorer.

As she dreamed of her future career, Biruté trained in ballet. Dance helped her develop patience, perseverance, and commitment. The physical stamina that Biruté later needed to travel through the rain forest began in childhood with the rigorous exercise program of a dance student.

As "New Canadians," her parents continually emphasized the value of education; they wanted their children to take advantage of everything available in this new country. When Biruté learned that a Ph.D. was the highest degree that a student could earn, she knew she must get one.

Left: From ballet class to the forests of Borneo, Biruté's parents were there to support her. Here, they pose with Biruté for a picture at the airport.

Right: Biruté, 12, participates in a ballet recital. Dance helped her develop key strengths that she would use to track orangutans through the rain forest.

As a young man, Rod Brindamour wanted to travel, and after he and Biruté married, he got his wish. Rod stayed in Borneo with Biruté for nearly a decade, helping her raise orangutans like Gundul (pictured) and maintaining their camp while Biruté carried out her observations. His photographs illustrated Biruté's articles for *National Geographic* magazine.

After spending a year at the University of British Columbia, Biruté enrolled in the University of California, Los Angeles (UCLA), to pursue a bachelor's degree in zoology and psychology. There she saw a photograph of a young male orangutan, one of the mysterious red apes of Asia, that mesmerized her. She was "fascinated by his humanlike appearance ... the relative flatness of his face, and the white surrounding the brown irises of his eyes." She found the gaze of the animal "almost hypnotic."

Biruté also met the person who would help her realize her dreams, Rod Brindamour, a handsome Canadian friend of her younger brother. The two became engaged within days after they met. Rod hoped to travel and explore the world; Biruté wanted to see orangutans. But first she had to figure out how.

Continuing graduate study in the anthropology department at UCLA, Biruté attempted to gain support from her professors to study wild orangutans. But no one there shared her enthusiasm for this course of action. Biruté had a plan for her life, but she needed help—a mentor to guide her along the way.

High Park

As the largest public park in the city of Toronto, High Park serves as an oasis from city life, where people can lounge under the beautiful black oak trees that turn red and orange-brown in the fall. This grand park houses lots of attractions—a zoo, a nature center, playgrounds, a dog park, restaurants, and more. As a child, Biruté loved to explore this beautiful natural setting.

HIGH PARK'S BENEFACTOR

After Europeans settled the area, a prominent architect named John George Howard bought the land where the park now sits and, eventually, donated it to the city of Toronto in 1876. In this agreement, Howard stipulated that the park remain as natural as possible, that the park's trees not be harvested for timber, and that the space would be open to everyone. Park guests can still visit the home and grave site of Howard and his wife.

AN UNTAMED PARK

Towering black oak trees, many of them around 150 years old, can be seen in the oak savannah habitat, one of the few examples still in existence in Ontario, Canada. To keep the area wild, downed trees have been left to decay and non-native species have been weeded out by volunteers at the park. There are several restoration sites located throughout the park, where dedicated volunteers keep the park's ecology in order. The result is a stunning green space beloved by Toronto's citizens.

WILD ANIMALS

In High Park, Biruté would have caught sight of many wild animals. At the 35-acre (14-ha) Grenadier Pond, visitors can glimpse beautiful birds such as swans, great egrets, and great blue herons; reptiles such as midland painted turtles and little brown snakes; and mammals like beavers and muskrat. The most common animal in the park is the chittering eastern gray squirrel, which actually appears in a variety of colors, including gray, black, and sometimes white.

ANCIENT HISTORY

High Park rests on land that was at different times inhabited by the Wendat, Haudenosaunee, and Mississauga peoples. Traces of indigenous history have been uncovered throughout Toronto, including evidence of long-houses and subterranean sweat lodges. Many artifacts have been found at archaeological sites in the city: pottery fragments, tools made of bone, pipe fragments, and marine shell beads (pictured).

"The whole world may be against you. The whole world may say that you are wrong. But I will always support you ... because *I* will know that you are right."

—comment from Louis Leakey to Biruté Mary Galdikas

MENTORS

The Influence of Louis Leakey
and Jane Goodall

Mentors, those who teach and help, often provide the
bridge from dreams to success. In Biruté's life, two people
made an extraordinary difference. She met the first, Louis
Leakey, in March 1969, when he presented a guest lecture at UCLA.
In his sixties, walking with a cane and missing most of his teeth, the
famed anthropologist, who had worked in East Africa to discover the
ancestors of humans, delivered his speech with a passion that moved
Biruté deeply. She felt he would have made "a great politician, a rabble-
rouser." While he was talking, he referred to a telegram he had just
received from Dian Fossey about her work with mountain gorillas.
He told the audience that the gorillas had become so comfortable
with Dian that one of them spent time untying her shoelaces.

Biruté and Rod pose for a picture with Louis Leakey (center). The famed anthropologist
helped Biruté secure funding so she could travel to Indonesia to study orangutans.

Louis Leakey and his family inspect the campsite of an early hominid during a 1961 excavation in Olduvai Gorge in Tanzania, Africa.

After the lecture, Biruté rushed up to Leakey. She told him about her enthusiasm for wild orangutans and about the people she had already contacted in Indonesia and Malaysia, home of the world's last remaining wild orangutan populations. Leakey took a long look at her and invited her to stay in contact and send him a letter when he returned to Africa. But by the time she arrived home, Leakey had called to make an appointment.

The next day, Biruté arrived at a home in California where Leakey was staying. He told her he wanted to give her some brainteasers, or intelligence tests, to learn more about her.

First, he spread out cards on a table. "Which ones are red and which ones are black?" he asked.

Biruté replied, "I don't know which are which, but half the cards are slightly bent and half are not."

Pleased that Biruté had noticed this difference, he mentioned that Jane Goodall could easily see the same thing, but that most men did not. Leakey had always insisted that women could observe things better than men and hence made the best scientists for fieldwork. After some conversation, he offered to find a way for Biruté to study orangutans in the wild, even if it would take some time for him to raise the money to finance her research.

Later he would tell her that he knew from the moment he met her that she would succeed in finding and studying orangutans.

Louis Leakey

The son of British missionary parents, Louis Leakey grew up in Kenya, a country in Africa. In 1921 he attended Cambridge University, in England, studying anthropology, archaeology, and African prehistory. After completing his studies, Leakey returned to Africa— to prove Charles Darwin's theory that human life originated there. And in 1948, Leakey and his wife, Mary, discovered the fossil remains of *Proconsul africanus*, an ancestor of apes and humans that lived more than 25 million years ago. Leakey and Mary continued their work at Olduvai Gorge in Tanzania, where they unearthed several famous fossils that helped scientists understand the development of the human and ape species.

Leakey's discoveries, including *Proconsul africanus* (upper left), proved that our origins were much older than the scientific community believed at the time, and that human evolution had begun in Africa. Posing for a photo, Leakey (right) holds some fossilized teeth he uncovered in Olduvai Gorge.

(Left to right) Dian Fossey, Jane Goodall, and Biruté Mary Galdikas broke barriers when they entered into the scientific community. In a field traditionally dominated by men, all three were encouraged by their mentor, Louis Leakey, and made discoveries that transformed the field of primatology.

Biruté waited in Los Angeles for two and a half years while Leakey worked to secure her funding. While volunteering at the Los Angeles Zoo, she spent hours observing orangutans in captivity. One day, when trying to entertain one of the females, Biruté slipped a nylon stocking to her; the animal put it over her face like a bank robber. The female attracted a crowd of hundreds of zoo-goers while walking around the enclosure and showing off her new mask. Spending time at the zoo only increased Biruté's desire to research these gentle, and sometimes silly, creatures in the wild.

In the summer of 1970, Biruté received an invitation from Leakey to join him in London, where he was staying in Jane Goodall's mother's flat. Biruté didn't want to miss this opportunity. She was completely in awe of Jane Goodall. For 10 years Jane had been studying chimpanzees in the wild. She'd made major breakthroughs in human understanding of these animals: They created and used tools, ate meat, and even practiced a type of warfare.

During that visit, Biruté also got to know Jane's son, nicknamed Grub; her husband, Hugo van Lawick; and her remarkable mother, Vanne Morris-Goodall.

Like everyone else who met Vanne, Biruté was impressed by this "spunky outgoing person who always had a twinkle in her eye." Biruté also appreciated how much Vanne had helped Jane in her work. The Tanzanian authorities would not allow Jane to travel unchaperoned into Africa in 1960 to begin her research, so Vanne volunteered to accompany her daughter. On the advice of Louis Leakey, Vanne provided medicine and basic treatment for those who lived in the area. Her efforts made it possible for Jane to be quickly accepted in the community and to spend her time in field research.

Unlike Vanne, Jane seemed a bit reserved and quiet; but when the discussion turned to chimpanzees, Jane lit up and became very funny.

At one point, Biruté turned to Jane and asked, "What am I going to do?"

"You're going to do exactly as I did," Jane replied. "You're going to go out and find them."

While Louis helped Biruté make preparations for her field study, Dian Fossey, the third of Leakey's protégées, arrived and presented Grub with a stuffed toy gorilla. It did not impress the young boy, who, after all, had been raised among wild chimpanzees.

Jane Goodall observed chimpanzees using tools during her field study in what is now Gombe National Park in Tanzania, Africa. Here Gimli, a young male, fishes for termites using a twig. This discovery, among Jane's many others, stunned the scientific community.

Spending time with these accomplished people, Biruté had a chance to observe how Leakey and his protégées acted. He slept on a mattress on a wood floor. They all washed their own dishes, laundered their own clothes, and carried their own suitcases. As Biruté noted: "There was a modesty about them," and they had not lost touch with reality—even though they had become very famous.

But Biruté still had to wait longer to "go out and find" orangutans. Finally, the Wilkie Brothers Foundation, the Jane and Justin Dart Foundation, and the National Geographic Society provided grants for her to develop the first comprehensive study of wild orangutans. At that time, naturalist John MacKinnon, who had worked with Jane Goodall at Gombe National Park, had conducted field research on orangutans for

The Great Apes

Great apes are our closest relatives in the animal kingdom and we share 98 percent of the same DNA. And like us, these amazing animals are extremely smart: They can use tools, show emotion, and think about abstract ideas. But each of the seven species of great ape is quite unique, with its own distinct features and characteristics.

Chimpanzees & Bonobos

Of all the apes, chimpanzees are the most like humans. They frequently use tools in the wild, hunt in organized groups, and communicate with one another through sounds and gestures. Bonobos—who share the genus *Pan* with chimpanzees—stand more upright than chimpanzees and live in more peaceful groups. Like gorillas, chimpanzees and bonobos can be found in African rain forests, as well as other wooded areas.

Chimpanzee

Bonobo

16 months. But still, scientists knew so little about these animals. Louis Leakey suggested that Biruté might need to stay in the field for at least 10 years to complete a study.

On September 1, 1971, Biruté and Rod began their journey across the world. In Washington, D.C., they stopped at the National Geographic offices and then flew to Africa to meet again with Louis Leakey and Jane Goodall. At Jane's research center in Tanzania at Gombe National Park, Biruté and Jane observed chimpanzees and Biruté learned techniques to locate wild animals and gather information about them.

Finally, Biruté's apprenticeship came to an end. Her next stop would be Indonesia—where she would endeavor to locate the elusive wild orangutans.

Orangutans

Covered in orange hair, which ranges from dark to light, orangutans spend most of their time in the canopy of the forest. They cling to trees and dine on fruits and leaves using their powerful arms, which are twice as long as their legs. The sole surviving great apes in Asia, three species of orangutans live only on two islands, Borneo and Sumatra.

Gorillas

Sometimes weighing more than 400 pounds (200 kg), gorillas are the largest of the great apes. They're also gentle giants known to live in family groups in the rain forests of Africa. Compared to their counterparts—western lowland gorillas—eastern mountain gorillas (pictured) have thicker fur to keep them warm.

The Trimates

Louis Leakey believed that studying primates in their natural habitats would be one of the keys to understanding human evolution. To do that work, he encouraged three female researchers, whom he called the Trimates (Jane Goodall, Dian Fossey, and Biruté Mary Galdikas), and raised funding for their research.

(Above) Jane Goodall visits with young chimpanzees at a sanctuary. Today, the Jane Goodall Foundation rescues and rehabilitates chimpanzees, and Jane advocates for the fair treatment of all animals.

JANE GOODALL

Even as a child Jane Goodall exhibited a passionate interest in animals. All creatures great and small—earthworms, dogs, chickens, or robins—fascinated her. In 1960, under the direction of Louis Leakey, she traveled to what is now Gombe National Park, in Tanzania, and began a more than 55-year study of wild chimpanzees. Over the course of her lifetime, she became the world's foremost expert on chimpanzees, one of the most recognized scientists in the world, and an advocate for conservation and animal rights.

(Above) Jane Goodall, who was only in her 20s when she started her groundbreaking study in Africa, holds hands with young Figan at her research camp in Gombe, Africa.

DIAN FOSSEY

A physical therapist by training, Dian Fossey borrowed money to take the dream trip of her life, a seven-week safari in Africa. On one of the final visits of the trip, she met Louis Leakey at his archaeological site Olduvai Gorge, in Tanzania. Later he found funds for her to establish a center to study mountain gorillas in Rwanda.

Fossey laid the groundwork for our basic knowledge of gorilla behavior and ecology, showed the world that gorillas were gentle giants—very different from the way they were portrayed in the past—and helped save mountain gorillas from extinction.

It took Dian months to even get close to the gorillas she was studying. But she eventually gained their trust by observing their behaviors—such as scratching, feeding, and knuckle-walking—and imitating them.

"The tropical rain forest is the most complex thing an ordinary human can experience on this planet. A walk in the rain forest is a walk into the mind of God."

—Biruté Mary Galdikas

CHAPTER 3

BORNEO

Exploring the Rain Forest

When Biruté and Rod's plane arrived in Indonesia's capital, Jakarta, she stumbled out of the air-conditioned jet and trudged through the heavy heat to the terminal. Random shouts filled the building as porters, customs officials, and passengers jostled for space. Dazed, Biruté and Rod picked up their backpacks to clear customs and then faced the chaos of taxi drivers honking and shouting. By the time they arrived at their hotel, "it was pitch black and raining hard." They ate their first meal at midnight in a coffee shop, the rain so loud they could barely hear each other.

A mother and baby orangutan climb through the trees near Camp Leakey in Tanjung Puting National Park. Young orangutans will stay by their mother's side for about eight years.

The first thing Biruté needed to do was secure a government permit to conduct her research. But when she met Walman Sinaga, the head of Indonesia's Nature Conservation and Wildlife Management Agency, he advised her against going to Sumatra, one of the 17,000 islands of Indonesia, where she had planned to work. Instead he recommended Tanjung Puting Reserve, in Borneo. The orangutans in that area had never been observed; hence, Biruté could be the first scientist to ever carry out field research there. He then placed Biruté and Rod under the care of a trusted member of his staff, who would escort them to their destination.

While travel arrangements were being made, Biruté and Rod picked up supplies in local markets. In one of them, Biruté purchased a durian, one of the favorite fruits of orangutans. Eating this stinky but tasty item would be the first of many experiments she conducted on the foods that some orangutans enjoyed.

Tourists photograph orangutans at a wildlife center in Borneo.

The Island of Borneo

The third largest island on Earth after Greenland and New Guinea, Borneo forms part of a string of islands that stretches between Asia and Australia, called the Malay Archipelago. It's also home to one of the oldest rain forests in the world, around 140 million years old.

Dutch and British explorers fought for control of the area from the 16th through 19th centuries and then, during World War II, Japan invaded. After the war, what was once called the Dutch East Indies became the independent country of Indonesia. Two-thirds of Borneo eventually became part of the newly formed country. The rest of the island is actually divided among two other countries: Malaysia and Brunei.

Because of its remoteness, few Westerners had traveled to Borneo when Biruté and Rod went in 1971. In Borneo, Biruté wrote "time had stood still." In recent years, because Biruté helped establish ecotourism as one of the main industries in central Borneo, visitors from around the world have been able to see the rain forests and orangutans who drew her to the island.

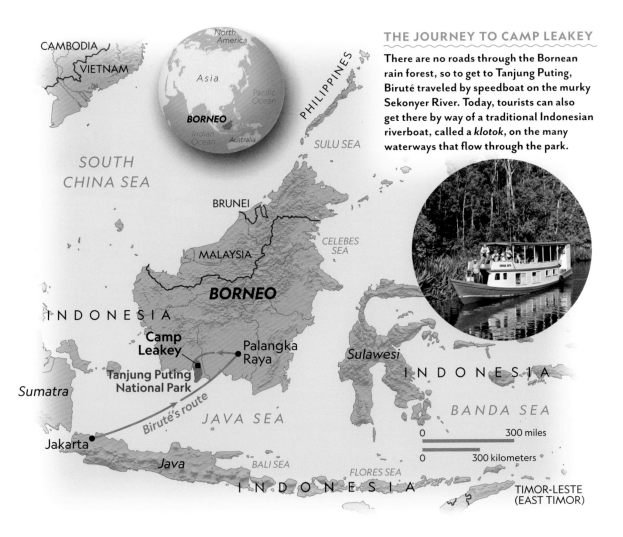

CAMBODIA
VIETNAM
North America
Asia
Pacific Ocean
BORNEO
Indian Ocean
Australia
PHILIPPINES
SULU SEA
SOUTH CHINA SEA
BRUNEI
CELEBES SEA
MALAYSIA
BORNEO
INDONESIA
Camp Leakey
Palangka Raya
Tanjung Puting National Park
Sulawesi
INDONESIA
Sumatra
Biruté's route
JAVA SEA
BANDA SEA
Jakarta
Java
BALI SEA
FLORES SEA
INDONESIA
TIMOR-LESTE (EAST TIMOR)
0   300 miles
0   300 kilometers

THE JOURNEY TO CAMP LEAKEY

There are no roads through the Bornean rain forest, so to get to Tanjung Puting, Biruté traveled by speedboat on the murky Sekonyer River. Today, tourists can also get there by way of a traditional Indonesian riverboat, called a *klotok*, on the many waterways that flow through the park.

After about a month in Jakarta and the nearby city of Bogor, Biruté and Rod boarded another plane to reach Borneo, a remote island that had few visitors. When they reached the provincial capital of Palangka Raya, with paved roads and concrete buildings, Biruté and Rod had to meet more officials and attend a party thrown in their honor. At the event, those present were expected to offer a rendition of their favorite song. Not particularly gifted musicians, the couple grappled with this unfamiliar custom, and she and Rod crooned their way through "Jingle Bells." Their efforts did not seem to impress the crowd.

After many hot and humid weeks in Indonesia, Biruté and Rod placed all their belongings in two small speedboats and headed south on the Kumai River and then east on a small tributary, the Sekonyer River, a black waterway the color of diluted Coke.

The orangutans Biruté and Rod would rescue were so energetic they took a toll on the small, bark-hut home. Eventually the couple was able to build a slightly more ape-proof wood home next door. They added a garden, and Rod cut trails through the dense undergrowth so Biruté could easily access her research site.

The driver raced through the twists and turns, causing water to pour into the boat and drench them. After several hours, Biruté and Rod parted ways with the speedboat and transferred into small dugout canoes, paddling during steady rain. They then passed through several lakes before the thoroughly soaked couple arrived at their final location.

In a place untouched by the modern world (there were no telephones, roads, electricity, television, or mail service) stood a small chocolate-brown thatched-roof hut. Biruté named her new home Camp Leakey in honor of her mentor. Located near the river, this temporary shelter, with only one small window, was theirs. Immediately she familiarized herself with the area. As she quickly learned, it held terrible dangers for human beings.

Mosquitoes, sand flies, and elephant flies stalked Biruté and Rod.

Poisonous caterpillars dropped from the canopy.

Tiger leeches, marked by a yellow stripe down their backs, located their prey with heat sensors and attached themselves to Biruté with tiny razor-sharp teeth.

Long-snouted crocodiles lurked in the water.

Large wolf spiders and fire ants left the comfort of the forest to invade the hut.

Pied hornbills cried. Cicadas, shrill and excited, made the rain forest vibrate with their calls and sounded like a jet plane ready to take off.

The Heavenly Durian Fruit

The size of a volleyball, the durian looks a bit like a dinosaur covered with sharp spikes. According to Biruté, the creamy yellow flesh smelled like rotten onions but tasted a bit like custard sweetened with almonds. Biruté initially found the skunklike smell horrible, and just opening a durian for the first time gave her a headache.

At night, if Biruté got up to go to the bathroom or get a drink of water, she often saw a snake slithering across the floor or felt its vibrating tongue on her hand.

And sometimes long after dark, a creature with shaggy red hair gave "a long series of deep and terrifying roars." An orangutan!

Even with its dangers, the rain forest thrilled Biruté. Everywhere she turned, she felt like she had entered the land of Oz, a magical place of new, unexplored sights. Millions of species, many rare, packed themselves into the rain forest.

Biruté experienced this land while living off very little money. Louis Leakey had initially managed to raise a few thousand dollars for their work. That meant they lived on very little—often with nothing to eat but rice, bananas, and sardines. Camp Leakey (with a roof that always leaked) served as their only home for years. They knew that eventually they would have to build a more permanent structure out of ironwood, which would not rot.

Leeches that feed on blood, like this Bornean tiger leech, are known as hematophagous leeches. They have a unique saliva that numbs pain and keeps blood from clotting, so that they can feed on animals without being noticed.

Leeches, Leeches, Everywhere ...

Borneo's leeches might look harmless, a bit like inchworms ... until they strike. These bloodsuckers blend into the undergrowth, standing rigid until prey passes close by. Once a meal is located, using specialized heat sensors, the leech raises a suckered end, and *chomp*. These "small Draculas of the rain forest," bite with intensity and suck blood until they are gruesomely swollen.

When Biruté and her husband, Rod, took off their clothes at night, fat black leeches "bloated with our blood ... fell out of our socks, dropped off our necks, and squirmed out of our underwear."

Two orangutans stop for a treetop snack. Orangutans eat mainly fruit, but they've also been known to dine on leaves, bark, flowers, and sometimes even insects.

In the meantime, they had to live in this less than ideal cabin, constantly invaded by the creatures of the rain forest.

For Biruté, the most frustrating of all the problems came not from her living situation or the wild creatures teeming around her, but from her inability to spot a single orangutan. As she and Rod, who served as photographer, manager, and fellow researcher, searched daily from dawn to dusk, the animals remained elusive. It took several days after they arrived to even catch a quick glimpse of one high in the trees.

Every day was a challenge. Biruté reflected, years later, "I would wade up to my armpits in the acidic, tea-colored swamp water, craning my neck to catch even a glimpse of the wild orangutans who traveled in the canopy created by the massive hundred-foot trees … I shivered from the coldness of the swamp water, my fingers and toes numb … my body raw from allergic reactions to the tannins and toxins in the water."

After a rainstorm, Sugito drapes a scarf over his head and offers his adoptive mother, Biruté, a kiss.

Biruté paddles a canoe through a waterway as Sugito curiously looks ahead. Most of Tanjung Puting is a low-lying tropical swamp, and the rivers and streams that cut through it all flow into the Java Sea.

Even though Biruté had a hard time spotting great apes in the wild, she saw orangutans illegally kept as pets. A week after her arrival, she encountered a baby male orangutan in a cage, captured after his mother had been shot. At her insistence, an Indonesian official confiscated the infant and motioned for Biruté to take him to Camp Leakey. Biruté felt lucky to have the little ape in her care. Orangutans do not often thrive in captivity, and he might have died. Biruté named her new orange-haired ward Sugito.

Raising Sugito, who had boundless curiosity, proved a bit more difficult than Biruté or Rod imagined. At first, the baby simply attacked them and bit whenever possible. Finally, Sugito seemed to decide that this strange, two-legged creature was as close to a mother as he could find. So he permanently attached himself to Biruté. He would scream when pried off and needed to be around her every moment, including when she slept. "As I walked, Sugito molded his body to mine … he clung to me."

For the first time, Biruté became a mother. She would later raise her own children in Indonesia, but Sugito became her first adopted offspring. As she explored the rain forest around her camp, Sugito wrapped himself around her neck "like a prickly red scarf." Changing clothes was difficult, because Sugito fiercely hung on to her garments. She even had to take baths in the river with him hanging on her body.

Although she found Sugito demanding, Biruté became enchanted by the baby. She loved the feel of his soft hair, so similar to human hair. Like a small child, Sugito loved playing with a knife and fork at the dinner table and enjoyed blowing out the candles at night. He gave her sloppy kisses and delighted in swiping her hats and clothes.

Little Sugito covers himself in tree branches. This kind of play helps him practice the skills he'll need to one day build a nest in the canopy—skills he couldn't develop if kept as a pet.

Akmad

At age two and a half, Akmad, a small dainty female, was rescued from a logging camp. Akmad was Biruté's first adopted orangutan daughter, arriving about a month after Biruté came to Camp Leakey in 1971.

Refined in her actions, she would reach for objects but never grab them like other orangutans. Even when she was given a package, she would open it gently and slowly, rather than ripping it to shreds like some of the more boisterous animals in the camp. Biruté described Akmad as the "gentle orangutan with the liquid brown eyes." Akmad demonstrated to Biruté just how individual these great apes could be.

Sugito hangs over Biruté like a scarf as she holds Yally, a gray gibbon. While Biruté's fieldwork focuses around orangutans, she also encounters some of Borneo's other wild inhabitants. Gibbons are smaller apes that, like orangutans, spend most of their lives in trees, swinging through the branches with their extra-long arms.

One by one, other formerly captive or orphaned orangutans arrived, and soon Biruté and Rod had a small family of furry orange creatures at Camp Leakey. Often Biruté felt as though she was "surrounded by wild, unruly children in orange suits who had not yet learned their manners. They used tools, liked to wear bits and pieces of clothing, loved to indulge in junk food and candies, were insatiably curious, wanted constant affection and attention, expressed emotions such as anger and

Two-year-old orangutans Sugito and Sobiarso clamor for their adoptive mother's attention. Wild young orangutans will cling to their mothers until they are four years old.

Cempaka

Cempaka came to live with Biruté after she had been held as a pet for seven years. Although orangutans in the wild have rarely been seen using tools, those in captivity often master a variety of them. Cempaka had a flair for sticks. She dug holes with them and would take one in each hand and use them to reach for plates and cups.

Cempaka often demonstrated just how effectively orangutans in captivity can mimic human behavior; she enjoyed eating at the table with forks or spoons. Mixing sugar, flour, and eggs in a glass, she practiced her own form of cooking, but was never allowed close to the stove.

embarrassment in a manner seemingly very similar to human beings." Like human children, they needed "lots of love and attention." These animals allowed Biruté to observe orangutan behavior—but their lives had been transformed because of contact with humans. Rehabilitating them to behave like animals who had lived only in the rain forest would later become part of Biruté's pioneering work with captive orangutans.

For her scientific work, Biruté needed to watch animals in the wild. Someone less determined than Biruté might easily have given up. Someone needing more comfort or more food would have headed back to civilization.

But Biruté Mary Galdikas had not spent years preparing to come to Borneo to turn back. She kept searching, and ultimately, her perseverance made all the difference.

The Heart of Borneo

With a booming population, the island of Borneo is undergoing enormous changes; human development and expansion encroach on its once untouched places. But one swath of rain forest remains intact. Called the Heart of Borneo, this incredibly biodiverse forest has developed a distinct ecosystem over hundreds of thousands of years, and it contains some of the world's most rare and unique animals, often found nowhere else on Earth. For the sake of those who call it home—and the entire ecosystem—protecting the Heart of Borneo is more important now than ever.

PYGMY ELEPHANT
(Elephas maximus sumatranus)

This petite pachyderm is about a fifth smaller than its Asian counterparts. Pygmy elephants have longer tails, round bodies, and are able to move freely through the rain forest without damaging the vegetation. Some experts believe that this subspecies might be descended from a group of now extinct Javan elephants originally brought to Borneo in the 17th century as a gift for the Sultan of Sulu. Today only 1,500 remain in the wild.

SUNDA CLOUDED LEOPARD
(Neofelis diardi)

Found only on the islands of Borneo and Sumatra, the Sunda clouded leopard was declared a new species in 2007. They typically sport small, distinct cloud-shaped markings. Scientists estimate that between 5,000 and 11,000 leopards live in the Heart of Borneo, where they exist as the island's top predators.

RED GIANT FLYING SQUIRREL *(Petaurista petaurista)*

Borneo is home to more than 10 species of flying squirrel—more than anywhere else in the world. Among these is the red giant flying squirrel. Like all flying squirrels, the red giant does not actually fly but uses a special membrane that extends from its wrists to its hind limbs to glide through the air.

SUMATRAN RHINOCEROS
(Dicerorhinus sumatrensis)

With short, bristly coats and two horns, Sumatran rhinoceroses are solitary creatures that browse their forest habitats, snacking on its vegetation. While they can weigh in at up to 2,100 pounds (950 kg), the Sumatran rhinoceros is actually the smallest of the world's five rhino species and one of the most endangered, with fewer than 100 left in the wild.

HELMETED HORNBILL
(Rhinoplax vigil)

The helmeted hornbill is the largest of all hornbills. It is named for the protrusion above its beak, called a casque, which it uses to "joust" over food or potential mates. Unfortunately, the hornbill, a critically endangered species, is hunted for its casque, which is made of a solid substance similar to ivory.

FLAT-HEADED FROG
(Barbourula kalimantanensis)

Small, squat, and with a muddy brown coloring, the Bornean flat-headed frog has no lungs. Instead, the amphibian gets its oxygen entirely through its skin. Scientists speculate that not having lungs might allow for this unique amphibian to sink more easily to the bottom of streams. However, water pollution from illegal gold mining is quickly becoming an enormous threat to the frog's survival.

"The orangutan is the hardest
of the great apes to study ... it takes
Biruté a year to gather information
and to see behaviors I might see
in one lucky day."

—Jane Goodall

CHAPTER 4

THE ELUSIVE ORANGUTAN

Finding the Animal With the Human Face

I n 1658 a Dutch physician described the orangutan as a "wonderful monster with a human face." In Indonesia, the indigenous people, the Dayaks, felt close affinity to this native animal. They called them orangutans: *Orang* means "person," and *hutan*, "forest." These "persons of the forest" have inspired many legends. In a version of the classic Beauty and the Beast story, an orangutan abducts a woman who is at first frightened but then realizes the ape is quite gentle.

Nestled among the dense foliage of the Bornean jungle, orangutans often slip by unnoticed, moving quietly through the trees.

Dayaks also expressed the belief that male orangutans are actually ghosts. Though they are certainly not invisible, seen within the dense rain forest, a mature male with cheek pads might appear to some to be a spirit because he moves without the slightest sound on the forest floor.

In their forest home, these shy animals prefer to go unnoticed. Because they usually travel through the canopy, Biruté had difficulty even spotting them and even more

The Dayak People

The native people of Borneo, the Dayaks, today consist of more than 50 indigenous groups living on the island. For centuries, the Dayaks preserved the rain forest by growing their food using a method known as shifting cultivation—clearing a patch of forest, planting crops with a stick, and then abandoning the area to move to another. This process allowed the forest to regenerate itself.

A Dayak man plays the sape, a popular instrument in Bornean culture. Traditionally, the instrument is played by plucking a melody on one string, while its other strings ring out in the background.

They also have an incredibly rich cultural heritage. Between their many ethnic groups on the island, the Dayaks speak 170 different languages and dialects—some by just a few hundred people. The traditional Dayak dance, the hornbill, is named after an iconic rain forest bird with a curved bill and brightly colored casque, or horn, on its head. Performed during the harvest festival and other celebrations, men and women dance to the sape, a type of lute. Today, Biruté employs many Dayaks in her research and rehabilitation centers. They work as medical personnel and managers of the camp, and they help raise, feed, and protect the orangutans as they get ready to be released back into the wild.

With their wide, flat cheek pads, male orangutans have a distinctive look. These pads, called flanges, help mature male orangutans attract females.

trouble following them through swamps. Inching along in the black water, Biruté would stop, look, and listen for a tiny noise, a leaf falling or branch breaking. The large lumbering animals managed to move almost silently through the trees.

For about two months Biruté spent day after day stalking the great apes. With a glass bottle of cold coffee, a notebook, a machete to chop down the brush, and binoculars, she traveled through the forest from dawn to dusk. But outside of distant sightings, Biruté had little to report.

One day, she finally caught enough of a glimpse to name her first animal, Alice. Just as Jane Goodall did, Biruté had decided to give the orangutans she met in the wild names, moving from *A* to *Z*. Jane had refused to follow the accepted scientific method of assigning numbers to animals, and Biruté believed in the wisdom of that approach. Each creature deserved to be treated like an individual with its own name.

Biruté had to look long and hard for orangutans, which spend about 90 percent of their time in the canopy. But she also listened closely for their distinctive calls. When threatened, orangutans may make a noise called a "kiss-squeak," and males often "long call" to alert other males to stay away—a sound that can be heard a little more than a mile (1.6 km) away.

Having spotted only one animal in two months, Biruté worried that she might have to leave this forest without obtaining much data on orangutans in their natural habitat. Still, day after day, she continued to search the rain forest.

Then, on Christmas Eve morning, Biruté finally had a breakthrough.

Rod had gone off to cut trails through the underbrush, and Biruté sat entering data in her notebook. Suddenly she heard a branch snapping. She whirled around and spotted an 80-pound (36-kg) female with an infant on her shoulder; even better, the pair did not run from her. The small fuzz-ball child stayed attached as the mother constructed a nest for daytime use. Then, moving slowly through the forest, she began to locate food to eat. The furry baby stayed on her shoulders, his arms wrapped around her neck. Biruté followed the two orangutans for an entire day—and named the pair Beth and Bert.

The next day, another miracle occurred. Biruté watched Beth and Bert emerge from their night nest. Seeing these two in the early morning was "the best Christmas present" Biruté had ever been given. All day she watched Beth, eating, moving, and then eating again. Bert noticed Biruté following and threw some bark at her. Then Biruté watched in amazement as Bert began to suck his thumb, just like a human child. While his mother worked to extract seeds from large prickly pods called *sindur*, a favorite of orangutans, Bert played with twigs. Moving from tree to tree at a leisurely pace, Beth spent the day foraging for food, nursing Bert, resting, and moving on. Much like sloths, Beth traveled in slow motion most of the time. With hips just as flexible as their shoulders, and two long hands and two feet that work like hooks, she crept through the

Building a Nest

Young orangutans need to learn how to build a new nest every night. At a sturdy spot—such as the crotch of a large tree (the spot where two branches or trunks have grown together to form a Y)—the animal bends the smaller branches of the limb into 90-degree angles to create a circular platform. The platform becomes the box springs of the nest. Then the orangutan spends up to half an hour collecting loose, leafy branches to pile on top, forming a type of leaf mattress. And because orangutans do not like rain, they sometimes make a canopy or roof of branches over the nest. In the end, the ape has made a comfortable, but small, nighttime sleeping spot. Young orangutans have to practice for several years until they get this formula just right.

Fifty feet (15 m) above the ground, three-year-old Subarno crafts a springy nest out of palm leaves. Orangutans are big fans of fresh bedding: Every night they construct new nests to sleep in. They also create new nests each time they nap, rarely reusing their old nests.

trees. On that truly memorable Christmas Day, Biruté had been able to watch all the movements of two orangutans. She was thrilled.

After three days, Beth entered the swamps, and Biruté had trouble following. Both the swamp and rain soaked Biruté, and she could not get dry. Covered with mosquito and gnat bites, she observed that her legs had turned bloody because of leech wounds. Although a walking physical disaster, Biruté only felt joy; she had observed wild orangutans in the field for 50 hours.

Then, on the fifth day of observation, Biruté felt a burning sensation on her buttocks. A huge black area of her skin appeared as if it had been burned to a crisp.

Throatpouch

A grouchy and difficult adult male, Throatpouch was named for his permanently inflated throatpouch, used for vocalizations. One day, deep in the jungle, Biruté watched Throatpouch react as he heard the call of another male orangutan nearby. Throatpouch prepared for battle. His hair bristled to make his size even larger. Had Throatpouch been a dragon, "he would have been breathing fire and chomping on horses."

The two males fought. Grabbing each other like sumo wrestlers, they bit each other, wrestled, and fell out of trees as they warred. Eventually, Throatpouch let out a spine-tingling roar and toppled a dead tree. His enemy vanished.

As the first scientist to see and document wild orangutan tool use and extensive adult male combat, Biruté found Throatpouch invaluable to her research. She watched the ape move along the ground, walking on the sides of his hands. He would drop from trees and claw for termites in the ground. Throatpouch even threatened Biruté and Rod at times; she later learned that he was "eight times as strong as a person."

At Camp Leakey, a mother shields herself and her baby from the rain with a leafy umbrella.

The day before, Biruté had sat on a wet log—and it contained poisonous sap. Now she could only lie on her stomach at night. That pain and her other injuries forced Biruté to return to her camp to recuperate.

Even after observing Beth, Biruté knew she had not made enough progress. Five months in the rain forests of Borneo had taken a toll on Biruté's health and on Rod's. They had eaten only rice, tinned sardines, and tea for months. Both had lost about 25 pounds (11 kg). They possessed only five sets of clothes, which they shared; because it rained almost constantly, the clothes often remained wet. "I was in swamp water all day, every day, dragging myself from one pool of slimy mud to the next." Biruté suffered from mysterious fevers and rashes. Her hands were so covered in tropical ulcers they were like claws. And when they became infected, she couldn't even close them into fists.

She began to feel that Louis Leakey had been right when he told her that a true orangutan study might take many years. The first five months had, at times, been torture.

An orangutan makes a ground nest. Bornean orangutans do sometimes travel on all fours along the forest floor. And when they need to rest, they make a temporary nest just like they do in the trees.

Fortunately, just at that point, she spotted another orangutan, Cara, who allowed Biruté to observe all kinds of behaviors that scientists did not know existed in orangutans. Cara's infant, Carl, threw branches at Biruté on their first meeting. Then a subadult male approached the pair and eventually began to wrestle and play with Carl. She watched the two great apes interact with each other. Now she knew that these animals were not as solitary as everyone believed.

Cara also showed Biruté how orangutans adapt objects for their own. One day in a heavy rain, Cara broke off two large leafy branches and held them above her head. Carl came to her side, and mother and son snuggled under this makeshift umbrella.

The longer Biruté stayed in the jungle, discovering the habits of her wild neighbors and studying them, the more critical data she gathered and the more she learned. In the next few years she would become the world's greatest orangutan expert because of her observations.

From 1971 to 1978, Biruté and Rod stayed in Borneo, making scientific breakthroughs in their quest to understand these Asian great apes. During this time, Biruté catalogued 400 types of orangutan foods (even gathering and tasting several hundred of the animals' favorite snacks herself); began to create family histories; mapped territories and home ranges of animals; and made observations about the social interactions of the animals in the wild.

No one had ever seen a wild orangutan sleeping on the ground, but Biruté saw one male do so for 45 minutes; later she located three ground nests, built on logs. As she worked on patterns of orangutan movement, she discovered that adult males prefer solitude. In 5,000 hours of study, only twice did she observe them interacting with each other.

The relationship between orangutan mothers and their children fascinated Biruté. Unlike other apes, like chimpanzees and gorillas, who might stay with their mothers for only a few years, a young orangutan will remain for at least eight. The reason for the extended childhood? The baby needs to be trained in everything—including what foods to eat and how to build a nest.

For the first six months of life, an orangutan baby stays glued to his or her mother for nursing. Then, after a year, the infant starts to explore a bit, but mom will still carry her child on her body for the first five years. Then, the youngster begins to travel behind the parent as she moves from tree to tree. If the mother leaves the sight of the young orangutan, the ape lets out high-pitched squeals. Training will go on for several years longer; the mother finds food and shares it with the child, eventually teaching the young orangutan to search alone. Only when the mother gives birth to another child does the first one leave her side.

Biruté had always been attracted to the calmness of adult orangutans. After studying the child-raising patterns of these mothers, she concluded that one of the reasons for

Biruté gathers wood at Camp Wilkie in 1973. She wrote that the construction of this outpost marked a "turning point" in her research as it allowed her much easier access to the rain forest where the orangutans roamed.

the serenity of the adults could be traced to their long childhood and protection by their mothers.

Although Biruté glimpsed females frequently, she never tired of seeing a male wandering in the wild. Still these males could be intimidating. When they spotted Biruté, they would frequently smack their lips as a warning and then hurl branches toward her.

Adult male orangutans possess huge cheek pads, giving them a large dish-like face that looks like they have "just stepped off a spaceship." And when a male makes his call, a throatpouch inflates to the size of a beach ball. "I wonder," Biruté wrote, "why people spend so much effort searching for intelligent life in space when there are such intelligent aliens right here on earth."

Living conditions gradually improved for Biruté and Rod. They built a new camp, which they named Camp Wilkie. Set up closer to the area where Biruté observed animals, it dramatically reduced the amount of time she needed to spend wading in swamps. This camp, constructed on a small platform with a thatched roof, had no walls. Soon they added a thatched-roof kitchen, where they cooked over an open fire.

In 1976 Biruté traveled to Jakarta to give birth to a son, Binti. Certainly, raising a child in the rain forest created unusual situations. With no other children around, Binti's first friends were wild animals, including Yally, a young gray female gibbon. Once Binti began to crawl, orangutans served as constant playmates. And Binti became particularly interested in using sign language with his new friends.

Like chimpanzees and gorillas, many orangutans show talent in learning sign language. Biruté invited graduate student Gary Shapiro from the University of Oklahoma to the camp because he had once coached Washoe the chimpanzee, a master at sign language. Gary and Biruté worked with two orangutans, Rinnie and Princess, who learned 20 signs in one year, a rate similar to the sign language superstars Koko the gorilla and Washoe. Princess actually learned 30 signs in two years of training, and she could combine them in short phrases. She used them to request food, grooming, and tickling.

For a period of time, Binti "signed with all the animals, even those who'd never been taught sign language."

As Binti grew older, both Biruté and Rod began to worry about the long-term effects of isolation from other children on their son. Biruté knew that her friend and

Princess

As Biruté's son Binti grew up, orangutans served as constant playmates. Once, as the young female, Princess, was getting a bath, Binti, with his clothes on, jumped into the tub. Then Princess climbed on his back.

Biruté considered Princess "bicultural" because she could fit into both the human world and the orangutan world. She learned to use dugout canoes "as portable bridges over swamps and streams," mastered locks in the camp, and loved to use combs and brushes to groom her hair. She also enjoyed washing clothes in the Sekonyer River.

Princess hangs onto Binti after he climbed into her bath. In this image, which appeared on the cover of *National Geographic* magazine, the young orangutan got a little closer to Binti than he'd bargained for.

Orange-haired students Unyuk (covering Biruté's eye) and Rio (leaning on Biruté's knee) gather around to observe one of Gary Shapiro's sign language lessons. During the lesson, Gary signs a question—"What's that?"—to which Rinnie the orangutan answers, "Tree." Orangutans are extremely intelligent and mastered many signs during Shapiro's lessons.

When Biruté's groundbreaking observations were detailed in the October 1975 issue of *National Geographic*, a now iconic image of her and two orangutans graced the cover.

mentor Jane Goodall had sent her son, Grub (born in Tanzania while Jane was conducting groundbreaking chimpanzee research), to England when it was time for his schooling to begin. After years in Borneo, Rod was tired of living in the rain forest and wanted to create a more traditional life. Sadly, Biruté agreed to a divorce because she realized that Rod could provide the needed comforts of civilization and education for their son. When Binti was ready for preschool, Rod returned with him to Canada.

Unlike Rod, Biruté did not want to leave Borneo—and the orangutans that she had found there. When she began her journey, Jane Goodall had told her that she needed to "find them" (the animals). Biruté found them and wrote up her research for her Ph.D. thesis and a groundbreaking article in *National Geographic* in 1975 that brought international attention to orangutans for the first time. But rather than seeking a full-time teaching position in a university, the usual course for a scientific researcher who has done fieldwork, Biruté found a part-time position at Simon Fraser University in Canada and became a tenured professor. She also chose to remain in Borneo much of the year, continuing her study of orangutans and expanding her research center.

In 1979 Biruté remarried. Pak Bohap bin Jalan, a member of the local Dayak tribe, shared Biruté's enthusiasm for tracking and learning about orangutans. He ran barefoot through the swamps, could pinpoint the source of any forest sound, and by just looking at bent twigs, could predict what animals had been in the area. Because Pak Bohap and Biruté were the first Western-Indonesian couple to marry in the province where they lived, it took four months to get government clearance for the wedding. They worked together on research, created their home in the area, and eventually had two children, Jane and Fred.

Science was the reason Biruté went to Borneo—but science was not why she stayed. Biruté truly loved the orangutans of Indonesia and learned to cherish the country she now called home. Because of her passion for orangutans, she turned Camp Leakey into the site of the longest continuous study of any primate conducted by one scientist. As she said in a documentary film about her life: "I came to Borneo looking for animals to study. I never thought I'd find lifelong friends."

As a child, Biruté's daughter, Jane, plays with young orangutans (right). Biruté and Pak Bohap care for their infant son, Fred (below).

Threats Orangutans Face

In recent decades, human activity has significantly threatened orangutans in Malaysia and Indonesia. Orangutans face many dangers, including from poachers, forest fires, and habitat loss due to timber and palm oil production. Both Sumatran and Bornean orangutans are critically endangered and are at risk of becoming extinct. Now, more than ever, it's important for conservationists to find ways for humans and orangutans to coexist.

HABITAT LOSS

Once found across Southeast Asia, orangutans now live exclusively on the islands of Borneo and Sumatra. Even within those islands, they live in small, fragmented groups. Several factors have caused orangutans' natural habitats to shrink over time—mining, unsustainable logging, and the creation of roads and human settlements through the rain forests.

FIRES

In order to make room for crops and plantations, farmers sometimes burn parts of existing forest. This technique for clearing land is called "slash and burn." In Indonesia and Borneo, it has been practiced illegally and without effective regulation, leading to fires that can grow out of control. These fires, worsened by drought and warming temperatures, have killed countless orangutans. The smoke that lingers after the fires, too, can lead to serious illness in both orangutans and nearby humans. Here, two formerly captive orangutans hang on to Biruté as she inspects damage from a fire.

PALM OIL

Palm oil, made from the fruit of the oil palm tree, can be found in all sorts of products people use every day—from shampoos to candy bars. Because of the commercial demand for palm oil, much of orangutans' native rain forests have been destroyed, to make room for more plantations. On a recent trip, Biruté drove seven hours over land covered with palm oil plantations before she finally saw scrub forest. As she says, "We have to save what remains for wild orangutans."

"Remember that in camp the orangutans come FIRST, science second, local staff and people third, and we, the foreign researchers, LAST."

—Biruté's rule for life at Camp Leakey

CHAPTER 5

THE FUTURE

Saving the Orangutans and the Rain Forest

When Biruté arrived in Borneo in 1971, the island was almost untouched. She later compared it to a Garden of Eden. But over time, Biruté saw changes sweep through the country as Indonesia entered the global economy. An influx of logging decimated thousands of acres of rain forest as land was cleared for palm oil plantations, mineral mines, and timber to make pulp and paper. People cleared forests across the island and built plantations in their place. This development produced large amounts of dry branches and other debris—perfect kindling for igniting destructive fires that burned nearby forests.

Caretakers from the Orangutan Care Center carry young orangutans who have been rescued from the pet trade, illness, and injury to a sanctuary. There, the orangutans will live, play, and grow their survival skills until they can be released back into the wild.

Biruté sits on a Camp Leakey dock among orangutans and gibbons, basking in sunlight and good company.

Over the years, Biruté and her staff have fought the fires themselves. In 2015, an extremely dry year brought brutal blazes that they fought for four months: "Our lungs still have not recovered from breathing smoke so heavy that sometimes you couldn't see your hand if you stretched it out in front of you." Finally, the rains came and extinguished the fires. But not before they devastated the orangutan population; the status of the Bornean orangutan changed from "endangered" to "critically endangered."

Biruté and her team have also had to contend with poachers who constantly invaded Tanjung Puting looking to take animals for the illegal pet trade or to hunt them. For years Biruté organized and led police patrols into the forest and swamps to make arrests. She started to receive death threats and for three years the Indonesian government provided around-the-clock protection for Biruté. Two armed police sergeants followed her every step, making sure she was not harmed.

Despite the dangers, Biruté did not hesitate to make her concerns known to the government. She confronted politicians, asking them to do more to protect orangutans and their forest homes. As Biruté noted in the foreword to this book, "If following wild orangutans in the swamps had not taught me patience, endlessly sitting in the waiting rooms of cabinet ministers and ambassadors, seeking appointments, certainly did."

Eventually, the threats inside the park from poachers lessened and Biruté no longer needed an armed guard. Yet, the battle to save orangutans and their habitat is far from over. Year after year as her study and rehabilitations continue, there are new issues to fight for to protect this critical rain forest species.

Every year about 15,000 lucky ecotourists travel to Biruté's home in Borneo to see the animals and terrain. Usually in small groups, they get to experience firsthand "the only place in the world where humans and great apes are truly equal." There are now 14 release camps, of which 3 are open to the public, including Camp Leakey.

Making a long river trip on wooden boats, powered by small diesel engines, guests take in the breathtaking rain forests and move slowly through the twisting waterways before they dock at the camp. There, curious orangutans wait for them.

Often Siswi, the Camp Ambassador, greets them first. A very friendly creature, Siswi loves being the center of attention and poses for photographs. She will roll around on the jetty, her legs waving in the air.

Using New Technology to Save Orangutans

While field scientists today may still hear the same "dental-drill sound of cicadas" that greeted Biruté in the Bornean rain forest, they can now conduct their research with the help of modern technology. Working with GPS units, tablets, and laptop computers, they follow orangutans—noting what they do, eat, and how they interact with others.

While Biruté was able to make astounding observations by tracking orangutans from the forest floor, today she and her staff can follow orangutans almost silently through the skies using drones. Cameras are attached to small aerial vehicles that can follow these elusive animals as they travel through the rain forest canopy or other rugged terrain that would be inaccessible on two feet. Conservationists can use the photos and video to study the effects of deforestation from above, images they'd never be able to get from the ground. And best of all, drones rarely disturb the apes' natural behaviors, allowing scientists to study them and quickly process research like never before.

Siswi

As the first surviving orangutan born in Camp Leakey in 1978, Siswi has learned all manner of things from humans, including how to sweep the kitchen with a broom and hold a bright pink umbrella over her head.

Siswi also appears to have developed an understanding of language. One day while eating a watermelon, she heard the rangers refer to "Dr. Galdikas," who was expected to arrive that day. Siswi ran down to the dock to hunt for Biruté. When she didn't find her friend, Siswi returned to eating the watermelon.

Visitors can hear lectures at the education center and watch animals feeding and swinging through the trees for hours. In the past, visitors had to fend off playful orangutans who wanted to "borrow" clothing items and other prizes such as camera film. Today that kind of interaction is rare because most of the rambunctious youngsters have grown up and have been released far from the camp. But a gigantic adult male may occasionally appear. In this amazing setting, visitors enjoy a once-in-a lifetime experience as they observe the workings of Camp Leakey and the animals who call it home.

Inspired by Dian Fossey, who found a way to save mountain gorillas through ecotourism, Biruté constructed feeding stations so that local inhabitants could observe the animals. As the business grew, the people of the area found employment, built houses, and prospered—as those from all over the world came to Camp Leakey to witness Biruté Mary Galdikas's legacy firsthand.

As a newcomer to orangutan research, Biruté discarded the accepted wisdom that she should work exclusively with wild animals. All around her, she saw captive creatures

Young orangutans play in the trees of Tanjung Puting to the delight of visitors at Camp Leakey. In 1985, Tanjung Puting was named a national park by the Indonesian government, helping protect these critically endangered apes.

A young orangutan lounges at the Orangutan Care Center. The residents of OCCQ are susceptible to disease, so the few visitors allowed to enter wear medical masks and undergo tests to make sure no contaminants are introduced to the young apes.

she wanted to rescue. She insisted on taking this action, even though the scientific community did not think it should be a priority. But keeping any orangutan she found alive seemed natural to Biruté. Initially providing sanctuary for orangutans allowed Biruté to observe their behaviors.

But her experience with them ultimately led to her discovering the best practices for preparing them to return to the wild. After a lot of experimentation, she settled upon an ideal formula for feeding captive young orangutans; she learned what they needed in terms of attention and care by humans. By raising many orphans, Biruté Mary Galdikas developed a program that sadly will be necessary in the 21st century to keep this magnificent creature alive.

In 1998, Biruté, as president of Orangutan Foundation International, established the Orangutan Care Center and Quarantine (OCCQ) facility for orphaned and ex-captive orangutans. All new animals undergo 30 days of quarantine and are tested for diseases like tuberculosis, malaria, and hepatitis. Parasites must be removed.

Then, after 30 days, the animals are placed in groups along with others of their age. Since animals in the wild live with their mothers for eight years, young orphan orangutans each get one or two human caretakers, supervised by Biruté. The orangutan will stay attached to the person, who remains with them, sleeps with them, and provides the constant attention they would receive in the wild. In the OCCQ more than 200 local people are employed and trained by Biruté to provide successful care for the orangutans.

Some of these orphaned orangutans require many years of living in the facility before they will be successful in the wild. All have to learn how to

Young orangutans practice their climbing skills in the OCCQ's forest. The skills they learn here will help them thrive once they've been released back into the wild.

Orangutan Foundation International

In 1986 Biruté founded the Orangutan Foundation International (OFI) to "support the conservation, protection, and understanding of orangutans and their rain forest habitat." The organization helps in the care of ex-captive and orphaned orangutans so they can be prepared for release in the wild. Working both to educate local individuals, as well as those worldwide, OFI provides employment for local Indonesians. Under Biruté's supervision, local Indonesians help continue the long-term study of wild orangutans as well as patrol local forests. They also work to restore areas destroyed by devastating fires. In just the past few years, OFI has planted thousands of trees in an effort to replenish rain forest habitat for all wildlife.

A staff member at OCCQ bottle feeds a one-year-old orangutan. Baby orangutans require a very specific diet to keep them healthy.

Tapanuli Orangutans

Until recently, biologists divided the existing orangutan population into two distinct species, Bornean and Sumatran orangutans. The two split apart about 600,000 years ago and have evolved separately. But there was one population of great apes in northern Sumatra that mystified scientists: a small group of about 800 orangutans living in the Batang Toru forest—an area measuring only about 425 square miles (1,100 sq km). Instead of just being a tiny population of Sumatran orangutans, scientists realized that this group is actually more closely related to those on the island of Borneo.

After examining a skeleton of one of these orangutans, completing a study of orangutan genes, and analyzing species behavior and habitat differences, researchers made an exciting discovery: That strange population on Sumatra was actually a separate species of orangutan, and the oldest of the three lineages. At first glance, the new group, dubbed *Pongo tapanuliensis*, or Tapanuli orangutans, may not look too different from their Bornean and Sumatran cousins. However, there are some key differences: Tapanuli orangutans have frizzier hair and darker fur; some males have more prominent mustaches while the females have beards; and males' skulls are slightly smaller than those of the other species.

All orangutans are critically endangered, but Tapanuli orangutans are probably the rarest and most threatened of all seven species of great apes. With the new discovery, conservationists like Biruté hope that the attention drawn to it will help efforts to protect and save all living orangutans.

Sumatran

A mother and baby Sumatran orangutan sit together in a tree. Like this pair, other Sumatran orangutans have bright, fiery orange fur.

Bornean

Although they spend most of their lives in trees, Bornean orangutans are sometimes found on the forest floor, unlike their Sumatran counterparts.

make nests and how to forage for and prepare food for eating. They first learn to swing on jungle gyms before they are introduced to the forest canopy. Daily supervised outings in the rain forest form a critical part of their rehabilitation. Biruté's facility became a model for similar centers in Sumatra, where Indonesian students study and rehabilitate orangutans using Biruté's methods. In their early stages, the various programs had successfully returned 800 animals to the wild. For this critically endangered species, every life counts.

During her career, Biruté has always refused to use research methods if she believed they might hurt any orangutan. At one point, a scientist wanted to assist her by putting radio collars on the animals so that they could be tracked. But this procedure meant that a certain number of them would die. Biruté refused to work with those who put science before the well-being of the animals.

Biruté has contributed invaluable records of what she learned in Borneo—including a meticulously researched 300-page doctoral dissertation, scholarly papers, two cover

A baby orangutan plays under a towel at the OCCQ, watched closely by a human caregiver.

Biruté poses with Mimi, a young orangutan. When Mimi was brought to the Care Center, she struggled to survive. But Biruté and the OCCQ staff worked hard to give her special care so that she could not only survive, but thrive as well.

stories for *National Geographic* magazine, two photography books, and her autobiography, *Reflections of Eden*. These publications changed the way the world and the scientific community view orangutans and their behavior. But some claimed that Biruté needed to publish more articles and more textbooks about her research. Often without these types of publications, grants dry up and scientists have to spend more time hunting for sources of money. But just as she has done with so many other things, Biruté refuses to give into such pressures. The animals, she argues, come before scientific journals.

Instead, Biruté has dedicated her time to teaching others about primate behavior, the tropical rain forest, and the plight of her beloved orangutans. As a permanent, part-time faculty member of Simon Fraser University in British Columbia, Canada, Biruté returns from the field for a few months each year to inspire the next generation of scientists. Unlike most animal researchers, she never left her area of study. She always returns to Borneo to observe and to rehabilitate animals. While there, she works with those who live in the area, to train them for work in her Orangutan Care Center.

In her work to save the rain forests, Biruté remains realistic: She understands that orangutans have been slowly vanishing. When people ask her, "What have you accomplished?" she always says, "We saved a wild orangutan population from extinction for almost 50 years."

When Biruté looks back over that time, she thinks about her suffering: "the malaria, the typhoid, hands that I couldn't use, of course that was bad. But the really hard struggle is keeping wild orangutan populations from vanishing. The last wild orangutan would be a male, making a long call in the forests of Borneo—with no one to answer his calls. I don't want that to happen."

But Biruté Mary Galdikas has never given up or given in—to physical pain, massive challenges, or despair. As she has said, "I'm fighting for the wild orangutan populations so that they will continue to exist in the wild and so the process of evolution continues unimpeded in them ... I have to keep going. That is the battle I cannot stop ... And I am going to fight that fight until the day I die." As a child, Biruté Mary Galdikas fell in love with nature and the stories of a very curious monkey. As an adult, she continues to be the best advocate and friend that orangutans, those "persons of the forest," have ever had.

The Lives She Touches

For nearly 50 years, Biruté Mary Galdikas has encouraged people around the globe, young and old, to act to save the environment and protect animals. Camp Leakey in Borneo has become a destination for people to see conservation in action, while Biruté's classes at Simon Fraser University serve to motivate students to change the world. Here are five stories—one from her lifelong mentor, three from people she inspired, and another from a student, all of whom were impacted by Biruté's work and passion for conservation.

DR. JANE GOODALL, DBE
Founder, the Jane Goodall Institute
United Nations Messenger of Peace

"How fortunate that Leakey helped Biruté Galdikas achieve her dream of working with orangutans in Indonesia. She succeeded in collecting fascinating data on their behavior despite the extraordinarily tough conditions she encountered in their forest habitat. Her subsequent work to protect them led to some ugly confrontations with loggers representing powerful vested interests—which would have caused a less dedicated and courageous person to quit. And she led the way in raising awareness around the world about the destruction of the rain forest habitat and the illicit wildlife trade which are bringing the species to the brink of extinction. She has, without doubt, saved the lives of many orangutans, particularly the orphans in her rehabilitation center. And, best of all, she has educated the local community, and inspired people around the world to become involved."

JANIE DUBMAN
Student, Simon Fraser University
Founding Member of OFI Canada

A student at Simon Fraser University, Janie Dubman was so inspired by Biruté's lectures that her career path was forever changed: "No other teacher has come close to the impact that Dr. Biruté Mary Galdikas has had on my life. Going far beyond the lectures and assignments of most professors, Dr. Galdikas shared her knowledge through unforgettable stories and firsthand experience. Allowing me to witness her life's work with the orangutans and the rain forest in Borneo opened my eyes wider than any book, and shaped my beliefs, plans, and dreams for the rest of my life."

IRENE SPENCER
Travel Designer for OFI Eco Tours

Ms. Spencer has been sharing the beauty of Borneo with tourists across the globe for more than 15 years, calling it "one of the most rewarding things in my life. These trips change people's lives in so many ways. After going on them, many people change careers or go in a different direction because of Dr. Galdikas. It is my joy to see people's reactions when orangutans come in from the trees and their expressions when they see the babies. They are absolutely awestruck, and the animals bring tears to many. Because Dr. Galdikas allows us into her life and shares her incredible stories and her devotion to the orangutans, we have all been changed by contact with her."

SY MONTGOMERY
Naturalist and Best-Selling Author

Author Sy Montgomery knew she wanted her first book to be about the three women she admired most: Jane Goodall, Dian Fossey, and Biruté Mary Galdikas. To research her heroines, Montgomery traveled where each worked and walked in their footsteps. While staying at Camp Leakey more than 30 years ago, she recalls, "Biruté has always made the training of Indonesian students a top priority at her camp. Several of her former students now serve in the Indonesian government; others are teaching at local universities; one served as an adviser to a cabinet minister and founded a prominent Indonesian nature conservation foundation. ... [Borneo] was an Eden filled with both demons (poachers and some politicians) and angels (all of the orangutans). To her credit, Biruté worked with them all."

DR. PATRICIA WRIGHT
Distinguished Professor of Anthropology at Stony Brook University

Dr. Wright combined her scientific study of lemurs in Madagascar with her work to preserve the country's forests. She was the driving force behind the creation of Ranomafana National Park in southeastern Madagascar, which is home to many endangered species. "Biruté has been a hero to me since the 1970s. She inspired me to believe I could go to the rain forest too. She brought attention to the conservation of orangutans. Biruté is amazing!"

FIELD NOTES
Resources and More

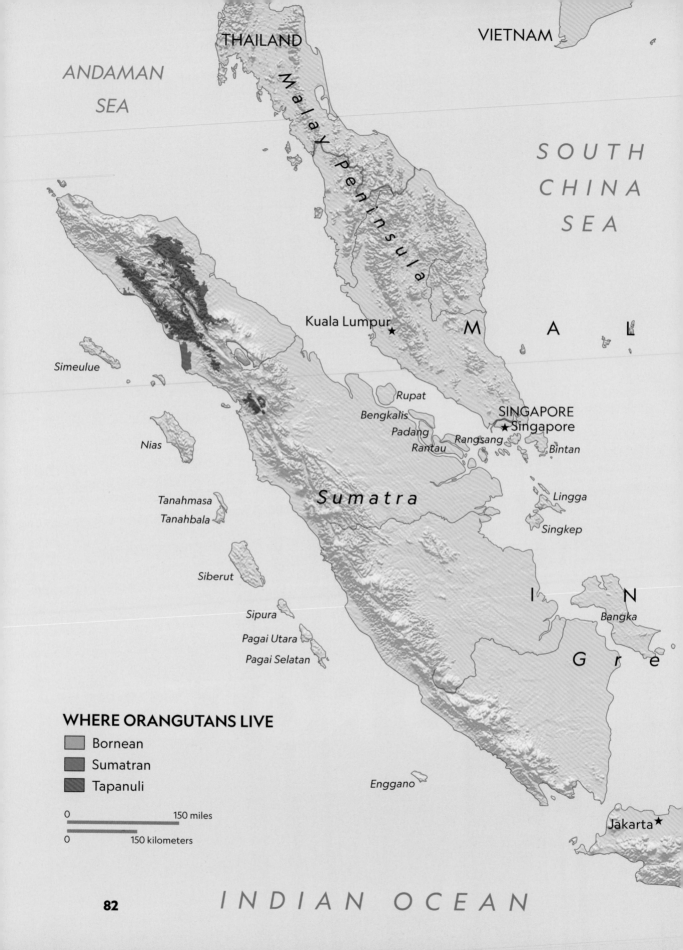

ANDAMAN
SEA

THAILAND

VIETNAM

SOUTH
CHINA
SEA

Malay Peninsula

Simeulue

Kuala Lumpur ★

M   A   L   I

Rupat

Bengkalis

Nias

Padang

Rantau

Rangsang

SINGAPORE
★ Singapore

Bintan

Tanahmasa
Tanahbala

Sumatra

Lingga

Singkep

Siberut

I   N

Sipura

Bangka

Pagai Utara

Pagai Selatan

G   r   e

WHERE ORANGUTANS LIVE

Bornean

Sumatran

Tapanuli

Enggano

Jakarta ★

0   150 miles

0   150 kilometers

82

INDIAN OCEAN

Orangutan Family Scrapbook

Sobiarso

This cheerful and lively orangutan was one of the first infants to live with Biruté in Borneo and constantly clung to her as if she were her mother. Sobiarso loved to put things on her head (such as the milk pan pictured here) and could also drink from the river while hanging upside down. When Biruté left Camp Leakey to teach in North America, Sobiarso disappeared into the wild.

Percy

Now in his late teens, Percy is slowly growing into adulthood and will eventually develop the signature cheek pads of mature males. Though small for an orangutan his age, he has a quirky and friendly disposition and spends the majority of his time traveling independently, though he occasionally returns to the Camp Leakey feeding station for food. Biruté is curious to see how long it will take for him to transition into a full adult male orangutan.

Andrena

Orphaned at a young age, Andrena blossomed into an energetic, kind, and agile young orangutan at Camp Leakey. She enjoys climbing trees and acrobatically swings through them for hours. Researchers hope that this long-haired, independent, and spirited orangutan will be able to return to the wild when she is a bit older.

Gina

Gina's mother, Gara, was rescued by Biruté. After her release into the forest, Gara went back to the wild without fuss, hanging out with several other young ex-captive females her own age. In 1987 she gave birth to her first infant, Gina, who now has children of her own. On one memorable occasion, when Biruté was alone in the forest, the adolescent Gina, who had always been aloof, spied Biruté and came over to initiate play. For Biruté, "it showed that Gina was happy in the forest, that she accepted me, and had adjusted well to life in the wild without her mother. Those are the moments I treasure."

Thor

Born in 2009, Thor is the sole surviving twin at the Camp Leakey study area. Independent and cautious, Thor disappeared into the wild when his mother died, but now visits to feed and play with his older brother, the sub-adult male Thomas.

Tom

Known to locals as the "King," Tom has been the dominant adult male in the forest around Camp Leakey for many years after defeating Kusasi in an epic fight. Along with his size, confidence, and lack of fear of humans, Tom is also known for being good-natured and easygoing.

Kusasi

Kusasi, a 300-pound (136-kg) orang-utan, was the reigning dominant male at Camp Leakey for about a decade until Tom defeated him in an epic battle. After losing his throne, Kusasi eventually left Camp Leakey. He was spotted months later, miles away from his old haunts.

Pan

Unlike the many rescues at Camp Leakey, Pan was born in the wild. An elusive traveler, Pan, who is Percy's older brother, only occasionally visits Camp Leakey to check in rather than to eat food. Pan's wandering ways are typical of male orangutans; females stay close to their mothers for years.

THE LIFE OF BIRUTÉ MARY GALDIKAS: A Time Line

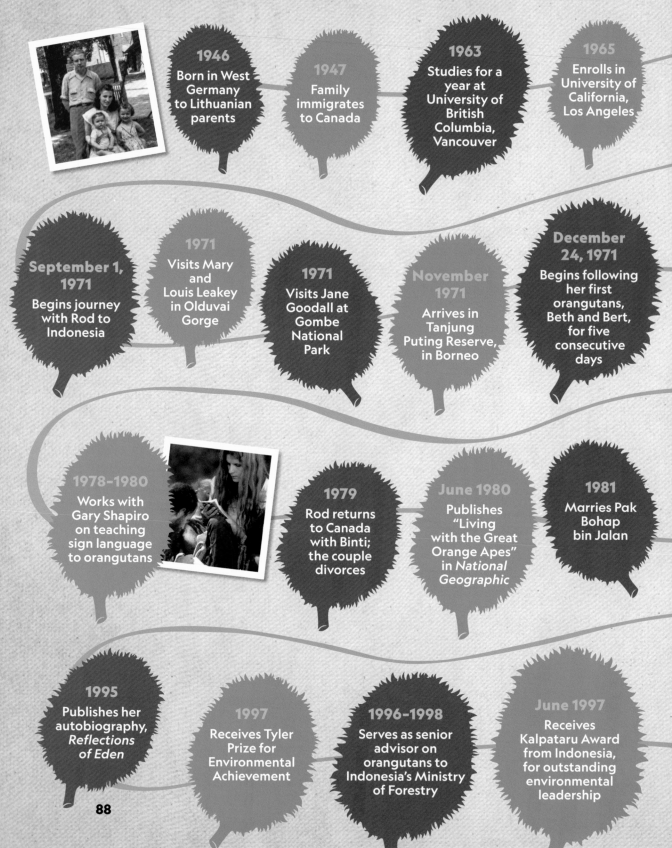

1946 Born in West Germany to Lithuanian parents

1947 Family immigrates to Canada

1963 Studies for a year at University of British Columbia, Vancouver

1965 Enrolls in University of California, Los Angeles

September 1, 1971 Begins journey with Rod to Indonesia

1971 Visits Mary and Louis Leakey in Olduvai Gorge

1971 Visits Jane Goodall at Gombe National Park

November 1971 Arrives in Tanjung Puting Reserve, in Borneo

December 24, 1971 Begins following her first orangutans, Beth and Bert, for five consecutive days

1978–1980 Works with Gary Shapiro on teaching sign language to orangutans

1979 Rod returns to Canada with Binti; the couple divorces

June 1980 Publishes "Living with the Great Orange Apes" in *National Geographic*

1981 Marries Pak Bohap bin Jalan

1995 Publishes her autobiography, *Reflections of Eden*

1997 Receives Tyler Prize for Environmental Achievement

1996–1998 Serves as senior advisor on orangutans to Indonesia's Ministry of Forestry

June 1997 Receives Kalpataru Award from Indonesia, for outstanding environmental leadership

1966
Receives bachelor's in psychology and zoology from UCLA

March 1969
Meets Louis Leakey, a guest lecturer at UCLA

1969
Receives master's in anthropology from UCLA

1969
Marries Rod Brindamour

Summer 1970
Visits Jane Goodall and Louis Leakey in London

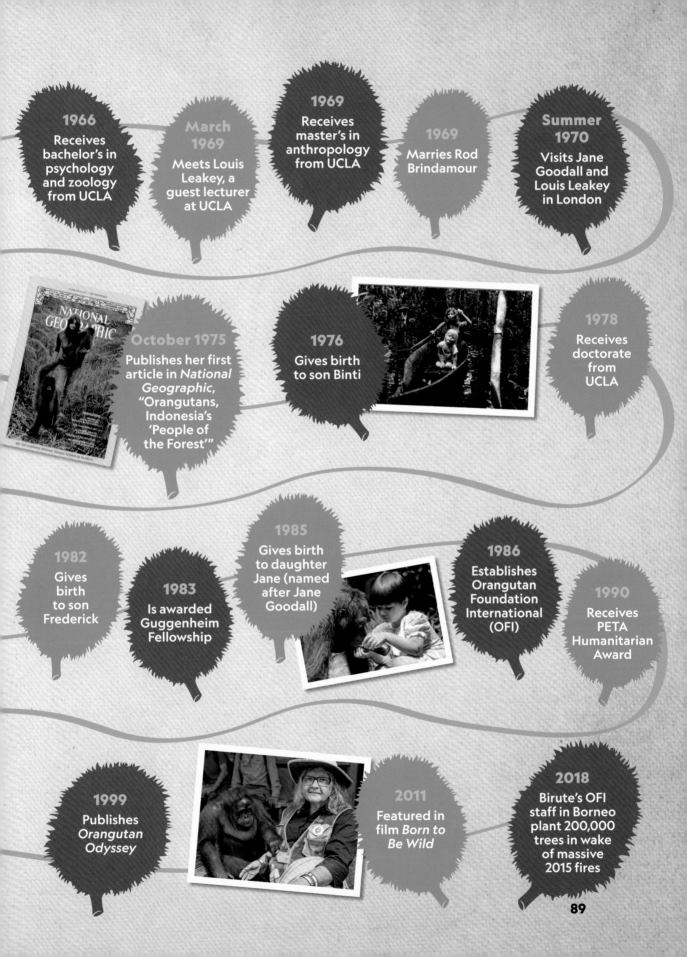

October 1975
Publishes her first article in *National Geographic*, "Orangutans, Indonesia's 'People of the Forest'"

1976
Gives birth to son Binti

1978
Receives doctorate from UCLA

1982
Gives birth to son Frederick

1983
Is awarded Guggenheim Fellowship

1985
Gives birth to daughter Jane (named after Jane Goodall)

1986
Establishes Orangutan Foundation International (OFI)

1990
Receives PETA Humanitarian Award

1999
Publishes *Orangutan Odyssey*

2011
Featured in film *Born to Be Wild*

2018
Birute's OFI staff in Borneo plant 200,000 trees in wake of massive 2015 fires

Key to Pictured Plants

Plants found in Indonesian Borneo are important resources for orangutans and their habitat alike. With uses ranging from sustenance to tools, Borneo florae are entities of both beauty and utility. While some plants are more prevalent than others, these featured examples are all essential to Borneo's thriving ecosystem.

Nepenthes rafflesiana

Also known as pitcher plants, these tube-shaped carnivores secrete nectar to attract prey such as insects and small rodents. Borneo contains the highest diversity of tropical pitcher plants in the world, about 80 known species.

Eusideroxylon zwageri

When studying orangutans, Dr. Galdikas observed a few individuals using the dead branches of this leafy tree as tools. One orangutan used a stick to scratch himself, while another used a branch to drive away pestering wasps. Humans also use the tree—known as ironwood—for construction, due to its ability to resist rot for long periods of time, even when standing in the watery swamp of the Bornean rain forest. However, this use has led to a decline in its population.

Ficus vasculosa

One of the more than 150 different types of fig tree found in Borneo, this species—called "bulu-bulu" by locals—has broad, veined leaves and round, golden fruits. Figs are an important food source for animals all across Borneo, including the rare hornbill.

Nephelium ramboutan-ake

This evergreen tree produces one of the orangutans' favorite snacks: an edible fruit covered by a hard, red shell and short, stubby spines, known as wild rambutan. The fruit is said to be both sweet and sour, similar to a grape. Humans also value the fruit for its medicinal properties, such as pain relief.

Campnosperma coriaceum

Known as "terantang" to locals, this large evergreen tree can grow up to 120 feet (40 m) tall, and sports yellow flowers when in bloom. Orangutans sometimes use the long, waxy leaves to line their nests.

Paphiopedilum kolopakingii

Borneo is renowned for its orchids, many of which are endemic to the island. One of more than 3,000 species found across Borneo, this particular type of orchid can only be found in Kalimantan.

Baccaurea pendula

In a study by Dr. Galdikas, she argued that orangutans help shape their own habitats by eating fruits and expelling their seeds in different areas of the forest. One tree that benefits from this is *Baccaurea pendula*, also known as *Baccaurea minor*, and to locals as "jijantik," which produces round, fleshy fruits. Orangutans tend to either swallow the seeds whole or spit them out, dispersing the seeds throughout the rain forest. They also sometimes carry the fruits or entire branches with their hands and feet, hanging onto them to snack on later.

Durio excelsus

Despite its scent—said to resemble that of rotting meat or old gym socks—durian is a favorite snack among orangutans, and often among people, too! The fruit, which has a mild, sweet, custard-like flavor, is used in both sweet and savory dishes. A mature fruit is approximately the size of a volleyball and grows on tall trees that can reach up to 130 feet (40 m) high.

Further Resources

Orangutans may be the most endangered ape on Earth, but conservationists and scientists like Biruté are working hard to make sure these great apes have a future for years to come.

BOOKS BY DR. BIRUTÉ MARY GALDIKAS

Galdikas, Biruté M. F. *Reflections of Eden: My Years With the Orangutans of Borneo.* New York: Little Brown, 1995.

Galdikas, Biruté M. F., and Nancy Briggs. *Orangutan Odyssey.* New York: Abrams, 1999.

Galdikas, Biruté M. F. *Great Ape Odyssey.* New York: Abrams, 2005.

OTHER BOOKS

Gallardo, Evelyn. *Among the Orangutans: The Biruté Galdikas Story.* San Francisco: Chronicle Books, 1993.

Laman, Tim, and Cheryl Knott. *Face to Face With Orangutans.* Washington, D.C.: National Geographic, 2009.

MacKinnon, John. *In Search of the Red Ape.* New York: Holt, 1974.

Montgomery, Sy. *Walking With the Great Apes: Jane Goodall, Dian Fossey, Biruté Galdikas.* Boston: Houghton Mifflin, 1991.

Nichols, Michael, Jane Goodall, George B. Schaller, and Mary G. Smith. *The Great Apes: Between Two Worlds.* Washington, D.C.: National Geographic, 1993.

Ottaviani, Jim, and Maris Wicks. *Primates: The Fearless Science of Jane Goodall, Dian Fossey, and Biruté Galdikas.* New York: First Second, 2013.

ARTICLES

Galdikas, Biruté M. "Indonesia's 'People of the Forest.'" *National Geographic.* October 1975.

Galdikas, Biruté M. "Living with the Great Orange Apes." *National Geographic.* June 1980.

White, Mel. "Out on a Limb." *National Geographic.* December 2016.

ONLINE

Discover more about orangutans with National Geographic Kids: *natgeokids.com/orangutan*

Learn more about Biruté and her groundbreaking foundation, Orangutan Foundation International: *orangutan.org*

FILMS AND TELEVISION

Born to Be Wild. Narrated by Morgan Freeman. IMAX 2011.

Mission Critical. "Orangutan on the Edge." S. E2. Original air date: April 22, 2016. National Geographic WILD.

Notes

Chapter 1: Explorer in Training

10 "As far back as I can remember..." Biruté M. Galdikas, *Reflections of Eden*, 19.

11 "I was born to study ..." Biruté M. Galdikas, *Reflections of Eden*, 33.

12 "Every week we went ..." Biruté M. Galdikas in discussion with the author, October 2, 2017.

15 "there is more than one way ..." Sy Montgomery, *Walking with Great Apes*, 11.

17 "We'd be walking ..." Biruté M. Galdikas in discussion with the author, October 2, 2017.

19 "fascinated by his humanlike appearance ..." Biruté M. Galdikas, *Reflections of Eden*, 43.

19 "almost hypnotic" Kelly Dinardo, "An Orangutan Expert Says Now Is the Time to Visit Indonesia," *New York Times*, December 29, 2016, nyti.ms/2hvDU8A.

Chapter 2: Mentors

22 "The whole world may...." Biruté M. Galdikas, *Reflections of Eden*, 95.

23 "a great politician ..." Biruté M. Galdikas, *Reflections of Eden*, 47.

24 "'Which ones are red ..." and "'I don't know which ..." Biruté M. Galdikas, *Reflections of Eden*, 49.

27 "spunky outgoing person ..." Biruté M. Galdikas, *Reflections of Eden*, 54.

27 "'What am I going to DO? ..." Sy Montgomery, *Walking with Great Apes*, 144.

28 "There was a modesty ..." Biruté M. Galdikas, *Reflections of Eden*, 57.

28 "go out and find them" Sy Montgomery, *Walking with Great Apes*, 144.

Chapter 3: Borneo

32 "The tropical rain forest is ..." Biruté M. Galdikas, *Reflections of Eden*, 91.

33 "it was pitch black ..." Biruté M. Galdikas, *Reflections of Eden*, 68.

34 "time had stood still" Biruté M. Galdikas, *Reflections of Eden*, 72–73.

38 "a long series of deep and terrifying roars" John Mackinnon, *In Search of the Red Ape*, 15.

38 "small Draculas of the rain forest" Biruté M. Galdikas, *Reflections of Eden*, 94.

38 "bloated with our blood ..." Biruté M. Galdikas, "Orangutans, Indonesia's 'People of the Forest,'" *National Geographic*, October 1975, 446.

40 "I would wade up to my armpits ..." Biruté M. Galdikas, *Reflections of Eden*, 87.

41 "As I walked, Sugito ..." Biruté M. Galdikas, *Reflections of Eden*, 128.

42 "like a prickly red scarf" Biruté M. Galdikas, *Reflections of Eden*, 139.

42 "the gentle orangutan ..." Gary Shapiro, "Orangutan of the Month: Akmad," Orangutan Foundation International (blog), November 14, 1999, orangutan.org/orangutan-of-the-month-akmad.

43 "surrounded by wild, unruly children ..." Biruté M. Galdikas, "Living With the Great Orange Apes," *National Geographic*, June 1980, 845.

45 "lots of love and attention" *Born to Be Wild*, IMAX, 2011.

Chapter 4: The Elusive Orangutan

48 "The orangutan is the hardest ..." Sy Montgomery, *Walking with Great Apes*, 149.

49 "wonderful monster with a human face" Sy Montgomery, *Walking with Great Apes*, 135.

53 "the best Christmas present" Biruté M. Galdikas, *Reflections of Eden*, 99.

54 "he would have been breathing fire ..." Biruté M. Galdikas, *Reflections of Eden*, 148.

55 "I was in swamp water ..." Biruté M. Galdikas, *Reflections of Eden*, 106.

59 "turning point" Biruté M. Galdikas, "Orangutans, Indonesia's 'People of the Forest,'" *National Geographic*, October 1975, 452.

59 "just stepped off a space ship" Biruté M. Galdikas, *Orangutan Odyssey*, 65.

59 "I often wonder ..." Biruté M. Galdikas, *Orangutan Odyssey*, 65.

60 "signed with all the animals ..." Claudia Dreifus, "Scientist at Work," *New York Times*, March 21, 2000, nyti.ms/2yv7Ffw.

60 "bi-cultural" and "as portable bridges ..." Biruté M. Galdikas, *Reflections of Eden*, 363.

63 "I came to Borneo looking ..." *Born to Be Wild*, IMAX, 2011.

65 "We have to save ..." Biruté M. Galdikas in discussion with the author, October 2, 2017.

Chapter 5: The Future

66 "Remember that in camp ..." Sy Montgomery, *Walking with Great Apes*, 159–160.

68 "Our lungs still have not ..." and "If following wild ..." Biruté M. Galdikas email correspondence, February 11, 2018.

69 "the only place in the world ..." *Born to Be Wild*, IMAX, 2011.

69 "dental-drill sound of cicadas" Mel White. "Out on a Limb" *National Geographic*, December 2016, 62.

77 "We saved a wild orangutan ..." and "the malaria, the typhoid, hands that ..." and "I'm fighting for the wild orangutan ..." Biruté M. Galdikas in discussion with the author, October 2, 2017.

78–79 Quotations from Dr. Jane Goodall, DBE, Janie Dubman, Irene Spencer, Sy Montgomery, and Dr. Patricia Wright, all in discussion with the author, August 2018.

84 Orangutan Family Scrapbook adapted from "Orangutan of the Month" profiles from Orangutan Foundation International and from email correspondence with Biruté M. Galdikas.

Index

Index

Index

PHOTO CREDITS

Author's Note

As I was working on my biography of Jane Goodall, *Untamed: The Wild Life of Jane Goodall,* I became fascinated with the youngest of Louis Leakey's mentees, scientist Biruté Mary Galdikas, once called "The Queen of the Orangutans."

Biruté's story amazed me. She had literally stayed in Borneo for nearly 50 years, living with and studying these animals. In Indonesia she married, raised children, and developed extensive ties with the government to help preserve orangutan land. She ignored basic scientific practices of the time and had taken orangutans rescued from captivity immediately into her camp. Her decisions in her first two decades of work—rehabilitating orphans, refusing to use invasive methods to study animals, and supporting her center with ecotourism—were forward-thinking and in tune with the best practices of 21st-century science.

But as incredible as I found Biruté's life, I learned that she herself is even more impressive to talk to and work with. She paid attention to the manuscript and pages and answered questions about her life and small details of her research—even though much of the time she was out of internet range in Borneo. Her thoroughness and her persistence were evident—no matter what the activity.

Books of quality nonfiction for children are essentially love letters to children from a lot of people. For this book I had the guidance of the best of all editors, Kate Hale, wise beyond her years. Kate works in harmony with her authors on every step of a book—from the outline to the final pages. Team *Undaunted*— including award-winning designer Marty Ittner; Sarah Mock, senior photo editor; Julide Dengel, art director; Joan Gossett, production editorial manager; Paige Towler and Kathryn Williams, associate editors; Avery Naughton, editorial assistant; and Mike McNey, the cartographer of these lovely maps—made the whole process of creating this book such a great experience. Laurie Hembree, senior product manager, and Bill O'Donnell, director of special sales, make publishing any book with National Geographic a joy.

In telling Biruté's story, I have also included portraits of orangutans themselves; after all, they kept Biruté in Borneo. I believe that Biruté Mary Galdikas can serve as a role model for any young person attracted to animals and science. She has given everything for her cause, has devoted all her talent and time to keeping orangutans alive, and has lived a life of meaning and purpose. I just hope that I have been able to capture her incredible story —so that it can be an inspiration for the next generation of scientists. —*Anita Silvey*